Sunny SOUTHSEA

MEMORIES OF A GOLDEN AGE

ANTHONY TRIGGS

HALSGROVE

First published in Great Britain in 2001
Reprinted 2007

British Library Cataloguing in Publication Data

A CIP record for this book is available from the British Library

ISBN 978 1 84114 106 0

HALSGROVE
Halsgrove House
Lower Moor Way
Tiverton Devon EX16 6SS
T: 01884 243242
F: 01884 243325
www.halsgrove.com

Printed in Great Britain by The Cromwell Press, Trowbridge.

Acknowledgements

So many friends and colleagues have helped with the production of this book, and I would like to thank those who have given their time and knowledge so willingly, starting with my publisher, Steven Pugsley, for his support. Researching pictures is the biggest part of any local history writer's work, so my thanks must go to those who have come to my aid – Tom Dethridge, Simon Evans, Rod Garnett, Roy Adams, Dave Garvey, Ray Moseley, and Bob Irwin of J.A. Hewes, Southsea, for his photographic skill and expertise. Finally my thanks go to my wife Sue for her help and encouragement, as always.

The railway poster featured on the back cover is reproduced courtesy of Dalkeith Publishing, Bournemouth. It is from one of the excellent sets of full-colour postcards on transport subjects they produce. A full list can be obtained by telephoning 01202 552352.

INTRODUCTION

Back in 1907 composer John Glover-Kind penned a song that was to epitomise a unique facet of English life. Although by now, nearly 100 years on, the verse has descended almost into obscurity, the chorus is still recognised and known by most people.

Oh! I do like to be beside the seaside
I do like to be beside the sea!
I do like to stroll upon the prom, prom, prom!
Where the brass bands play:
Tiddly-om-pom-pom.

These words conjure up images of late Victorian life – the promenade, the bandstand, Punch and Judy, fish and chips, candy floss – all of which are still surviving today.

Holidaymakers still take to the prom, enjoy eating ices, and continue to buy those souvenirs (don't ask!) which look great in the shops but are usually relegated to the loft on the return home.

Visitors still paddle in the sea and even fall asleep in deckchairs with knotted handkerchiefs on their collective heads.

However there are differences. In those early days a tantalising glimpse of a well-turned ankle would be guaranteed to set a young man's pulse racing, while nowadays a young lady almost wearing a tiny bikini would hardly merit a second glance.

The seaside resort was a successor to the inland spas, which had evolved over the centuries from the early religious pilgrimages to sources of holy water. Bathing itself first became popular in the 1720s, and the first bathing machines entered the sea at Scarborough in about 1735.

Victorians and Edwardians went to the seaside for the bracing air, not for the sun. It was only later on that a suntanned body was regarded as a sign of good health. Bathing in the sea was considered by the medical profession to be the cure for any ailment, and although in the better areas of the beach men and women had their own bathing huts and tents, in other parts nude mixed bathing was (surprisingly) perfectly acceptable until quite late in Victoria's long reign.

In the main the cumbersome costumes made privacy difficult, and bathing machines were only useful if you could afford one. The ordinary person would have changed on the beach, affording a great deal of amusement from the promenade for anyone who could afford a pair of opera glasses.

Southsea as a resort developed from the area created outside the town walls in the early nineteenth century, when businessmen and senior officers of the garrison fled the overcrowded and insanitary conditions for the more affluent and effluent-free locales.

Firstly they sought refuge in the magnificent terraces, but later went on to build the elegant and imposing villas with large grounds and stunning sea views.

An early guide book by the Old Portsmouth firm of Charpentier for Southsea and Portsmouth (note the predominance of Southsea) described the resort in glowing terms.

It read: 'Steeped in traditions of the past, envisaging the naval pageantry of the present, and sheltered by England's most lovely isle, there has arisen in the centre of the southern coast a great seaside health and pleasure resort – Southsea.'

With the coming of the railway to Portsmouth in 1847 Southsea became a magnet for a new breed of visitor – shop workers and factory staff taking their bank holidays 'at the seaside'.

As the influx of visitors increased then the entertainment on offer widened.

Southsea common, then owned by the War Department, offered the spectacle of military pageants and reviews, but this was not enough, and the town had to look to the future.

Clarence Pier was opened in 1861 with a capital of £4000 and by 1874 had been enlarged to cater for an expected 4000 visitors daily. The first South Parade Pier was opened in 1879 by Princess Edward of Saxe-Weimar and was considered to be more fashionable than its smaller brother. Both handled the steamer trade offering trips along the coast to Brighton and Weymouth, or journeys to the Isle of Wight.

By the early years of the twentieth century the corporation was looking to improve the resort even more to cater for the 'charabanc' parties that were beginning to invade the area. In 1922 the War Department sold Southsea common to the town, and the aldermen pledged £60,000 to convert it into gardens and playgrounds.

Provision was made for grass and hard tennis courts, a bowling green, putting green and football pitches. The gardens of the Ladies' Mile were developed during the winter of 1924-25 and by 1929 land to the west of Southsea Castle was given over to a children's area with a paddling pool, boating lake and miniature railway. And to add to the glamour more than 9000 coloured lights were festooned from Clarence Pier to South Parade Pier.

By 1938 the right to a paid holiday became law, and although the war put paid to any travelling, the visitors soon took advantage of new-found freedom in the '40s and '50s, when seaside resorts enjoyed the biggest boom ever.

Although in the '60s wider ownership of the car and the advent of television for entertainment changed people's leisure time, Southsea still attracted the visitors – even against the lure of the continental sunspots – and even now holds its own as a resort to be reckoned with.

The pictures in this collection will it is hoped provide an evocative look at a popular resort, and will perhaps give different perspective on a holiday spot which, come rain or shine, will always be known as Sunny Southsea.

Anthony Triggs,
Portchester, 2001

The resort of Southsea in its early days at the end of the nineteenth century with Beach Mansions to the right of the picture. The building still stands although now it is the Royal Beach Hotel. In the distance can be seen Southsea Castle.

The first South Parade Pier – the pride of Portsmouth – was opened on 26 July 1879, by Princess Edward of Saxe-Weimar, the wife of the lieutenant governor of the garrison. The 600-foot structure was then owned by Messrs Head, Wrightson and Company, a private firm whose shareholders included Edwin Galt, a former mayor of the town and a principal shareholder in the East Southsea Railway, and Albert Besant, brother of the novelist Sir Walter Besant.

On 14 July 1904, the unthinkable happened when the pier was engulfed in a blaze. The fire started after a long spell of hot weather and the timber was bone dry. A concert was in progress at the time and the audience made a rush for the doors, leaving the concert party, the Merry Makers, on stage. They too then made a hurried exit in a not-so-merry mood. The Ladies' Grecian Band of Harps, which was uninsured, lost all its instruments, which were being stored in the manager's office.

Following the devastation of South Parade Pier the corporation took control and undertook a rebuilding programme. Southsea photographer Stephen Cribb, a prolific postcard publisher, recorded this view of the aerial railway carrying construction materials from the mainland across the gap to the pier structure.

The fully-restored South Parade Pier was reopened to the public in 1908. This J. Welch postcard shows the newly-painted pier just before the official opening, with workmen's huts still standing on the beach, and one painter giving a final spruce-up to the railings at the bottom left of the picture.

Illuminated trams were often used to promote events in Portsmouth and Southsea, and here tram No 80 is decorated for the reopening of South Parade Pier. The wording in the lights on the side panel reads: 'Success'. The tram itself was fairly new having entered service in 1901.

The new South Parade Pier boasted a luxurious theatre, which over the years hosted many famous names. The theatre originally seated 1450, but following alterations to the stage, this was reduced to 1200.

An estimated 40,000 people crammed the beach at Southsea on 6 July 1912, when the *Daily Mail* waterplane arrived. The aircraft had left Hamble at 3.00pm and arrived at Southsea at 3.20pm to a cheer that was so loud that the pier band playing 'See the Conquering Hero Comes' could not be heard. Afterwards 36 people were taken on joy rides. The town was packed with people who had come for the fleet review, this time by members of parliament and not royalty, when 223 ships were assembled at Spithead.

A photographer was obviously a rare visitor to Margate Road, early in the century. This postcard by Southsea cameraman Charles Cozens clearly evokes the children's sense of wonder, and even the chicken wanted to get in the act.

Furs and hats were *de rigueur* at Clarence Pier at the turn of last century. The pier pavilion was a popular meeting place in the days when affairs of the heart had to be discreet.

A few years later a ticket collector takes payment for the hire of a deckchair on the beach near Clarence Pier. At the end of the pier passengers are boarding a paddle steamer bound for the Isle of Wight, or perhaps just for a leisurely cruise.

Swimsuits, towels and picnic baskets, along with their owners, are packed on the beach near Clarence Pier. Across the water is Gosport, with the spire of Holy Trinity Church just visible.

Albert Road in the days before the Kings Theatre was built. The line of buildings on the left of this Barkshire Brothers' postcard is identical today, while the police station on the right is now a public house. The Kings Theatre, designed by Frank Matcham, was opened in 1907.

Clarence Esplanade is shown in these two views with just a few years between them. The cannon remains the same and children still climb on it despite the warning notice. Dress is not a whole lot different but the mode of transport in the background gives the game away. In the earlier picture horse-drawn vehicles wait on the road, whereas they have been replaced with a different sort of horse-power in the later view.

Left: Horse tram No 66 awaits passengers at the junction of Clarendon Road and South Parade Pier. Local company Mumby's is advertising its mineral waters. By 1901 the horse trams had been superseded by electric trams. The trams were finally made redundant in 1936.

Below: Horses take refreshment as drivers await customers at the cab shelter on Southsea common. To the left of the group of four-wheelers, or growlers as they were known, can be seen a clutch of bath chairs, obviously available for hire to the more infirm visitors.

Clarence Pier was a favourite spot to pick up steamers. These two pictures are of an identical nature but with a time gap of about forty years. Right, decorous Victorians await the arrival of the *Duchess of Fife*, one of the Joint Railway Company's steamers. The company ran four more boats – the *Duchess of Kent*, the *Duchess of Norfolk*, the *Duchess of Albany* and the *Princess Margaret*. The slightly similar picture below shows the paddle steamer *Southsea* approaching the pier in about 1937. The main queue is for a cruise to Sandown, Shanklin and Ventnor, while the smaller group waits for a boat for a Solent cruise.

This page and opposite: The Trafalgar memorial on Clarence Esplanade, with its huge anchor, was always a popular subject for photographers as these four pictures show. The anchor is a replica of the original one, taken from Nelson's flagship *Victory*. The memorial was previously sited to the north of Clarence Pier, but was moved in 1880 with the redevelopment of the Assembly Rooms which once stood on the site. The monument even got a clean-up occasionally.

Above: Two members of the armed services watch workmen give the anchor a coat of paint within the enclosure of the cast-iron railings.

Because the common was originally owned by the War Department, the vast area was often used for military reviews. This Welch postcard, which would have been a good seller because of the number of military families in the area, shows the massed ranks watched by interested residents, including a few nannies and their prams.

A squadron of American warships visited Portsmouth in 1922, and on 18 June Vice-Admiral A. Niblack agreed to a request from the mayor, Albert Porter, that a band from his flagship, U.S.S. *Utah*, would play on the common. Crowds stood, sat on the grass, or relaxed in deckchairs as the musicians played. It is interesting to note there is hardly a bare head in sight.

The hotel is an important facet of any seaside resort. The opulent Queens Hotel (above) was a top destination, as was the Carlton (right). The latter became city council offices and has now been converted into residential flats and apartments. The Royal Beach (opposite top), opposite South Parade Pier, has still kept its identity and can be compared to the first picture in this collection. Near Clarence Pier stood the Esplanade Hotel (opposite bottom), built largely of timber. It could be pulled down easily if the guns of the garrison troops needed a clear view seawards, although thankfully this never happened, but German bombers finally sealed the fate of the hotel. Behind it was the fairground, then known as the Bijou Park.

It's not all fun and sun at Southsea – the winter months present a totally different perspective as these four pictures so graphically show. Rough seas pound the coastline leaving the promenade looking desolate and bleak and often bringing damage with them.

An intrepid photographer prepares his apparatus outside the newly-opened snack bar at Clarence Pier in 1932, while a balloon seller waits for customers. The ornate pavilion of the pier dominates the background.

One of a number of cards picked up at a postcard fair, this picture of day trippers dated August 1932 has been included more for its nostalgic charm than its historical content, although the hut in the background does indicate the City of Portsmouth car park.

Elm Grove was an elegant shopping area before the war. Many fine old houses had been demolished to build the shops, provoking a huge public outcry.

Snow and slush are still to be seen on Elm Grove in February 1931 as part of Southsea's history disappears. The felling of the elm trees which gave their name to the road sparked more outcry at what was called the desecration of the city, but despite that, the beautiful giants were removed.

Crowded beaches are not just a modern-day phenomenon as this tightly-packed picture from 1938 shows. Britain was not yet at war with Germany and the rolls of barbed wire and security fencing were still in the future. Swimmers brave the sea while the less hardy opt for a boat trip.

Lady bathers prepare to take to the waters early in the last century. Portsmouth Swimming Club was founded in 1875 and was later to become the largest of its kind in the country with almost 1500 members. Men and women each had their own area on the beach so as not to offend propriety.

Daring, or what? These ladies, with their fashionable headwear enjoy themselves in the waters at Southsea. Costumes were slowly allowing more skin to be shown, although it would be many years before swimmers would wear as little as they do now.

For a short while Southsea had its own railway. It was opened in July 1885 and ran for just under 2 miles from Fratton station to its own terminus at what is now Granada Road. The little line however could not compete with road transport and it closed after a mere twenty-nine years. An item of rolling stock is seen under the bridge in Albert Road, which is seen again in the second picture (below) from a different viewpoint with two cyclists and a delivery boy taking an obvious interest in the photographer.

People amble along the prom near South Parade Pier, while others relax on the pebble beach. The two little girls in the centre of the picture are carrying buckets and spades hopefully, while dad is expecting a swim if the towel rolled up under his arm is anything to go by.

A good life could be enjoyed with a bit of money in the balmy days between the wars. Apart from the vintage of the cars the reader could possibly mistake this view for one of today, with cars parked door to door on the common. The car park attendant in his white coat is collecting the cash in the midst of the cars at the right of the picture.

The shopping areas of Southsea were considered to be the best and highest class in the days before the war. Kings Road was one of the busiest and one of the oldest. The flags are out for one of the popular shopping weeks that attracted the crowds in the good old days. Flags are also out in Elm Grove (above) although these are in honour of the jubilee of George V and Queen Mary in 1935. In Palmerston Road Handleys' department store was the place to go for all your needs (below left), as was Knight and Lee's ornate store, (below right) pictured by St Andrew's Road photographer Stephen Cribb.

Electricity was the byword for two Southsea picture houses early last century, when cinemas were popping up all over the city. On 22 September 1911, the Southsea Electric in Fawcett Road opened its doors, offering luxury with free tea and biscuits to its balcony patrons. The cinema went through a number of identities, finally closing as The State in 1940. Nearby in Albert Road the Apollo Electric (opposite) opened a year later. The 'electric' part of its name was dropped soon after, but the cinema continued in business until November 1975.

King Neptune and his fishy cohorts prepare the mayor for the crossing of the line ceremony at Southsea carnival. Sadly Charles Cozens has omitted to put the date on his postcard, but nevertheless fun was surely being had by all.

Naval rating Arnold Roberts sent this undated postcard to his mother in Staffordshire. It shows the crew of his ship, H.M.S. *Kent*, performing the Gilbert and Sullivan operetta *H.M.S. Pinafore* at Southsea Castle. Patriotic Arnold ended his message to his mum with the words: God save the King.

Photographer Edgar Ward captured dancers tripping the light fantastic in the dark at South Parade Pier. The fairy lights and the music must have provided a great atmosphere for the participants on a summer's evening.

The paddling pool was situated next to the children's boating lake, near Southsea Castle. Parents could bring their youngsters and let them play in the shallow water in complete safety.

Above: Fun on the water at Southsea. In the picture a family enjoys a ride on the swan boats at the Canoe Lake. The boats provided a reminder of the swannery which used to be sited on the lake. **Below:** youngsters and parents become sailors for a short time at the children's boating pool near Southsea Castle.

Ice cream cornets could be bought for as little as one penny at the snack bar on Clarence Esplanade. This snapshot evokes a more leisurely way of life, and today's postcard collectors would no doubt like to get their hands on the dozens on offer in the racks.

Dancing was all the rage at Clarence Pier in the 1930s. For 3/6d you could dance until midnight – evening dress only – to the music of Hugh Frossard and his Broadcasting Band.

Education is taken for granted today, but things were a little different early last century. Standards were steadily improving, but schooldays could still be a bit spartan, as experienced by the little children of St Bernard's kindergarten, in Grove Road South (above). For older children it could be better, especially if a youngster possessed artistic talent. The art room of the Convent of the Cross Catholic High School in Grove Road North is full of classical ideas for budding artists (below). Finally a job lot in hairstyles was available to the young ladies of Ravenscourt, in Elm Grove. Ravenscourt was one of the four hostels belonging to the Portsmouth Ladies' Day Training College, (opposite) and is recorded here by Oscar Owers.

The elegant structure of South Parade Pier is clearly seen in this evocative picture. A tram is making its noisy way towards the pier, while a workman attends to a task with the help of a step ladder.

Southsea Castle provides a background to a bright afternoon walk. A walking stick and a hat are the necessary accessories for this pastime, while for nannies a cloche hat and a large pram are the thing.

Cottage Grove provided a mix of residential and business properties. The line of sun blinds evokes a past age, while the delivery boy giving his mate a lift would be frowned upon today.

On a summer's day South Parade Pier was like a magnet for visitors. Even in the 1930s lines of cars would be parked where Southdown buses would park in years to come. Walking along the prom was considered the thing to do, and even sitting on the seats to admire the view was acceptable.

Passengers disembark from a tram at the Ladies' Mile. Route numbers replaced the earlier letter code in July 1927, and the figure 4 shows the tram was on the round trip from the Dockyard to South Parade Pier, returning via Milton, the last village in Portsmouth.

Taking the sun was popular between the wars, although in those days the amount of clothing worn on the beach was far in excess of today's more relaxed dress. In the background are the booking offices for coach trips, organised by such operators as Royal Blue, Byngs, White Heather, Southdown, Triumph and Victoria.

With Southsea Castle in the background, navy crews man their whalers to compete for the Davis Memorial Trophy off Southsea.

These two pictures highlight a popular attraction on the Southsea seafront. The children's miniature railway was opened in 1924 near Southsea Castle and boasted three-quarters-of-a-mile of track, a station and a tunnel.

Fleet reviews were always a popular entertainment, with the pomp and royalty, and could be enjoyed from the shore or afloat. A crowd of steamer trippers enjoy the fun out amongst the warships gathered at Spithead for George V's Jubilee review in 1935.

Crowds pack the beach to see the royal yacht *Victoria and Albert* head for Spithead and the royal review of 1935. The ship was carrying King George V and Queen Mary and other members of the royal family. The King had arrived at Cosham railway station on July 15 together with the Prince of Wales, the Duke of York, and the Duke of Kent, and drove through 5 miles of cheering crowds to the dockyard where the party boarded the royal yacht.

A delivery boy rides his tricycle along Elm Grove. Some of the trees are still standing, and the spire of the Elm Grove Baptist Church dominates the skyline. The year is probably 1930 as the Scala cinema is showing *Hell's Angels*, released in that year.

These young dancers make a pretty line-up as they pose for the camera. The dancing school was situated near the Kings Theatre, perhaps a good position to get the young students places on the stage.

Cutting the grass makes Southsea common look spick and span, and here a tractor is being used to complete the springtime task.

South Parade Pier with its white pavilion roof stands out against the sea as the aerial cameraman makes his exposure. The tightly-packed houses of Southsea and the Canoe Lake are clearly highlighted.

Time for fun? The floral clock at Southsea was always a good crowd puller, especially in springtime when the parks department would ensure that the hours were recorded in abundant colour.

Anyone for tennis? A leisurely game is taking place at Clarence Parade, watched by a couple of spectators, or perhaps players awaiting their turn on the court. Behind is the ornate facade of the Queens Hotel, while the spire of St Thomas's Church, now Portsmouth Cathedral, is visible on the horizon.

The long arm of the law boasted luxurious accommodation in the '30s. This beautiful old house in Festing Grove was taken over by the police to form headquarters with a difference.

For many years this circular painting hung in The Barleymow public house at Southsea. It commemorated a series of events which started on 7 August 1874, which became known as the Glorious Battle of Southsea. The affair started when the local newspaper reported that the approach to the shore near the Southsea Pier (later Clarence Pier) had been barricaded by the Southsea Baths and Rooms Company. The situation gradually got out of hand until at the end crowds marched across the common to remove the offending planks of wood. Naval and military personnel, dockyard-men and navvies were joined by as many layabouts and the trouble started. The police and military were called in – the soldiers were armed with three rounds apiece – and gradually the mob was driven back across the common. Afterwards there were serious repercussions with many complaints of rough treatment by the police, who were armed with stout staves. Many of the participants are depicted on the painting.

The Second World War has hit Southsea, and the common is home for army gun emplacements. The Queens Hotel fills the background on the right as gunners prepare their equipment.

Southsea suffered badly in the blitz and many of the old buildings were lost to the German bombs. The evocative view of members of the Pioneer Corps pulling down a dangerous wall in Green Road clearly shows the devastation in the area. The picture (opposite top left) shows what was left of the Rev. Bruce Cornford's beautiful church of St Matthew in Fawcett Road after incendiary bombs fell on the roof and could not be reached. The church was restored after the war (opposite top right). Another of the pre-war shopping centres suffered, such as these shops at The Strand after high-explosive bombs fell. Lastly Stanley Street is strewn with wreckage after the Luftwaffe paid a visit (opposite bottom).

Left: The sad ruins of the Eye and Ear Hospital stand forlornly after the bombing of 1941. The hospital was opened in 1914 and gave its services to the city until the bombers came.

Below: The aftermath of the war is all too obvious in this unusual picture of Palmerston Road, looking towards the shopping centre. Marmion Road is on the left, out of view, while Kent Road turns off to the right.

Thomas Ellis Owen's St Jude's Church stands alone after the destruction of the blitz was cleared. This view was taken from Palmerston Road, with Kent Road running out to the left, behind the church. At first sight the picture could have been taken on the same day as the previous one, but the fact that the Kent Road sign is now high on its pole denotes a later date.

In order to tidy up some of the more ugly bomb sites, the city council transformed them into temporary gardens. In this picture a trolley bus picks up passengers as council workers put the finishing touches to the area where Handleys' department store stood. The store was eventually rebuilt and is now part of the Debenhams empire.

Handleys' rebuilding is well under way as shown in this rooftop shot along Palmerston Road. At the bottom of the picture Woolworths has already erected a sign to denote where its own new store is to be as the redevelopment of the shopping area starts.

The date is 11 September 1951, and crowds start to disperse after hearing the Lord Mayor of Portsmouth, Councillor Albert Johnson, declare open the first premises in the rebuilt shopping centre at Palmerston Road. The camera is facing towards Grove Road South.

On 6 June 1948, the fourth anniversary of D-Day, Field Marshal Bernard Montgomery was back in the city to unveil the D-Day memorial at Southsea. The ceremony was broadcast by the BBC. The simple block of concrete which forms the memorial was reminiscent of the anti-tank defences which were situated all along the south coast.

An Osborne Road shopper makes her way past the Cut Loaf restaurant, an eating place that came to be almost an institution in the city. The trolley buses were coming to the end of their service: the last one ran on 27 July 1963.

The Canoe Lake forms a backdrop to this picture taken from a high vantage point on the roof of a seafront hotel. A trolley bus – one of the silent service – moves away from the bus stop on the left while coaches await day-trippers on the right.

A snowy day at Southsea Terrace, pictured from the roof of one of the council offices, then situated in what was once the Carlton Hotel.

Spectators stop along Clarence Parade to see the might of the United States navy pass on 9 July 1947. The huge aircraft carrier U.S.S. *Randolph* had just been paying a ten-day visit along with the battle-ships *New Jersey* and *Wisconsin*.

Two years later more United States ships – a midshipmen's practice squadron – arrived in the city, headed by the giant battleship U.S.S. *Missouri*.

Lumps Fort was transferred to the city in 1932 and the old military establishment was transformed into rose gardens. In this picture the redundant gun emplacements are still visible.

Beach huts were put to good use by those who could afford them. You could sit in the sun, sunbathe on the grass, or just chat to your neighbour without the hurly-burly of the beach.

Lines of naval cadets watch the commander-in-chief Portsmouth, Admiral Sir Arthur Power, unveil the statue of Admiral Lord Nelson, on 11 July 1951. The memorial in Pembroke Gardens was presented to the city by Dr J. H. Aldous. During the civic procession to the opening ceremony the cathedral bells rang 630 changes of grandsire triples.

By the 1950s television had all but killed the typical seaside end-of-the-pier entertainment enjoyed by all before the war. This picture shows a sparse audience at South Parade Pier watching a band concert.

Cars and coaches fill a huge area of the common as this aerial view from August 1962 shows. The Queens Hotel is across the common to the right of the picture, while the spire of St Jude's stands high above the tightly-packed build-ings of Southsea.

A summer's day on the Ladies' Mile when deckchairs were the thing. Servicemen mix with civilians to take advantage of the fresh air and sun, with the camera obviously attracting some attention.

Watching the ships on the Solent has always been a pleasure, whether the vessels are large or small. A family enjoys the view in this picture from the early '50s – after the austerity of the war trips to the seaside were more easily available and affordable.

Right: Those interested in the larger ships were catered for by the noticeboard giving details of all the comings and goings. The United States battleship *New Jersey* on the list dates the picture at 1956. The huge vessel and her sister ship *Iowa* visited in April of that year.

Below: In July 1968 Portsmouth welcomed back a city explorer. Southsea greengrocer Alec Rose had sailed around the world single-handed in his yacht *Lively Lady*. People crowded the beach and little ships packed the water to show their support as he made landfall.

No, this is not a scene from the blitz. It's just the demolition of a Southsea landmark in May 1972. The Victoria Road Methodist Church was being demolished, the spire having been removed bit by bit to avoid injuring pedestrians, some of whom have stopped to watch the work.

Clarence Pier funfair offered colourful and noisy entertainment for young and old. The big wheel, removed in 2001, at 56ft 6ins was the tallest in the country at the time of opening in February 1964.

This aerial view from the 1970s shows the corner of Marmion Road and Palmerston Road, before the redevelopment of Marmion Road. The huge triangular area in the centre of the picture is now the Waitrose food store and car park.

Buses are parked around the area of gardens known as The Dell on South Parade in the late '50s or early '60s. There was always a pile-up of buses at this point with the various services leaving for different parts of the city and beyond.

An unusual view of the Southsea Castle complex with temporary buildings such as Nissen huts retaining the wartime feel. In the background the white building is the Rock Gardens Pavilion.

The craze of roller skating was considered fun and healthy at the rink on the common. For 1/- (5p) skaters could enjoy an hour's skating (skate hire was part of the deal) or for half that amount friends and loved ones could watch the inexperienced make fools of themselves.

Life in miniature was on hand at the model village at Lumps Fort. A young fan admires the oast houses and their small inhabitants.

In the '50s a new affluence returned after the austerity of the war. More people owned cars as is apparent from this picture. The horrors of the war were not forgotten, however, for on the far right work is going on to extend the naval war memorial to accommodate names of the fallen from the Second World War.

Cows on the common could be normal for a country village, but it is surely unusual for Southsea. The naval war memorial provides a stunning background as handlers move their charges around the show ring at the Royal Counties Agricultural Show in 1953.

It's the end of a bank holiday break and fun-seekers make their way homewards after a great day out at Southsea. On the common a number of cars are parked and a group of coaches wait to take excursionists back to their out-of-town homes.

What a jumbo job it is washing down baby elephants when the circus comes to town. Big-top handlers manoeuvre their young charges into the water at Southsea.

Water skis were still something to be looked at. People near South Parade Pier stop and watch the experts as they come into the shore.

Crowds line the seafront in August 1974 as smoke and flames belch from South Parade Pier, while firefighters battle to bring the blaze under control. The accident happened during the filming of the Ken Russell rock musical film *Tommy*, and damage estimated at £500,000 was sustained.

The white lady, as the pier was always known, looks somewhat desolate in 1975, a year after the fire. Work was commencing to bring the attraction back to life to once more give pleasure to residents and visitors alike.

Workmen cut down trees on Southsea common in December 1974 in an attempt to stop the spread of Dutch elm disease. The proud monsters had graced the common for years but were now reduced to unsightly stumps.

In October 1987 Southsea suffered when the great storm hit the south coast. Walls collapsed and trees were uprooted as this picture taken on Southsea common shows. Mighty trees that had been the pride of the city were lost in one dreadful night.

Another piece of cinematic history to disappear from Southsea was the stately Salon. The picture house was originally the Odeon, and was built in 1937. In its day it boasted seating for 1700 customers and had the largest car park in the city.

In July 1965 the traditional ferry service to the Isle of Wight was overtaken by the hovercraft, now the oldest service of its kind in the world. The windsock near the landing place at Clarence Pier flies high above the craft as it prepares to leave for Ryde.

Did the hovercraft really travel to the North Pole? We are excused from thinking this as Santa arrives at Southsea in December 1974. The red-coated favourite was on his way to his Aladdin's Cave attraction at Debenhams store at Southsea.

The Rock Gardens restaurant offered casual dining, with tables placed outside for al fresco eating during the summer months. The Rock Gardens themselves were usually filled with floral colour, although the small area included in this picture looks a little uninspiring.

Not so far back in history is this typical beach scene from the '60s, with double-decker buses awaiting passengers and a trolley bus making its way past the Savoy ballroom.

A strange juxtaposition of land and sea is apparent as the former royal yacht *Britannia* leaves Portsmouth for France in June 1994, the fiftieth anniversary of D-Day.

Southsea's soubriquet of sunny does not always apply as this stormy view from 1993 so eloquently depicts. A double-decker makes its way past the naval war memorial after leaving Clarence Pier on a wet and windy day.